POETIC INSPIRATIONS

POETIC INSPIRATIONS

Darron Hurst

Library of Congress Control Number:		2018914894
ISBN:	Hardcover	978-1-9845-7286-8
	Softcover	978-1-9845-7287-5
	eBook	978-1-9845-7330-8

New International Version (NIV)
Holy Bible, New International Version®, NIV® Copyright ©1973, 1978, 1984,
2011 by Biblica, Inc.® Used by permission. All rights reserved worldwide.

Print information available on the last page.

Rev. date: 01/18/2019

To order additional copies of this book, contact:
Xlibris
1-888-795-4274
www.Xlibris.com
Orders@Xlibris.com
787562

CONTENTS

DEDICATION

This book is dedicated to my Lord Jesus Christ, who is the source of all spiritual gifts and blessings; without His loving-kindness towards me down through the years, I truly don't know where I would be. I thank You, Lord Jesus, for showering Your rich grace upon such an unworthy sinner as me. I am eternally indebted to Your Love.

I also dedicate this project to my loving and devoted family: my beautiful wife, Miranda, who has faithfully stood by my side for the past twenty-six years and has always pushed me to reach my fullest potential; and my wonderful children, Darian, Jared, and Courtney, whose fearless pursuit of their personal goals and dreams has inspired me to courageously pursue my own.

And last but not least, I dedicate this project to the loving memory of the most devoted servant of God that I have ever witnessed, my beloved grandmother Mrs. Evelyn Nance. It was your steadfast faithfulness towards serving and honouring God that deeply impacted all aspects of my life; it serves as the basis of inspiration for my own desire to faithfully serve the Kingdom of our Lord!

FOREWORD

In the beginning was the Word and the Word was with God, and the Word was God, the same was in the beginning with God. All things were made by Him; and without Him was not anything made.

We believe this quotation from the Apostle John to be true, and yet we find ourselves still in awe and in amazement when viewing any newly divine creative works of God that's manifested through mankind.

Poetic Inspirations from Pastor D is a divinely written inspirational book of poetry and prose. Pastor Darron Hurst has uniquely crafted and exegeted God's Holy Word into inspirational prolific words of poetry. We understand that there is the *Word of Knowledge* presented to us by academia and then there is the *Word of Wisdom* presented to us by life's experiences, then there is the *Word of Revelation* revealed to us by God through the Holy Spirit. This *Word of Revelation* requires you to have a close relationship and connection with God. Pastor Darron Hurst has tapped into the revelation of God's Holy Writ and has masterfully penned this divine work of art.

Thank you, Pastor Hurst, for allowing God to reveal such masterful revelatory words of poetry that paint real-life pictures of relevance that inspire, uplift, and encourage. We applaud and celebrate you, Man of God, for this creative inspirational work.

Bishop Richard J. Pender Sr., Pastor
Beth-El Temple Church of Christ

PREFACE

Poetry has always had a profound effect on me. I remember how captivated I was as a little boy by the beauty and symmetry of various forms of poetic expressions. Poetry has the unique ability to create lasting impressions upon the mind while bringing simple language to life. I have found poetry to be comforting to the heart, soothing to the emotions, and inspirational to how we view and think about situations in our lives. The goal of this book of Spiritual Poetic Expressions is to bring to life various scriptural verses from the Bible, crafting them into poems that serve to highlight the inspirational messages contained in each verse. Through each poem, it is my hope that a visual portrait is created in the reader's mind that inspires renewed faith, hope, motivation, and perseverance amid the challenging ordeals and obstacles that life presents!

It is my sincere prayer that each Poetic Expression will unlock the true power of Inspiration that the Holy Scriptures were designed to accomplish in the lives of all whose hope and comfort are derived from the living Word of God!

I Can

So many of us are gifted to accomplish something truly special and influential in life, but often we are hesitant to try because of certain but unwarranted fears; this can be the fear of failure, the fear of inadequacy, or the fear that no one will believe in the viability of what we have to offer. This poem, "I Can," resonates a confidence that through faith in Christ and confidence in the gifts that He has graciously bestowed upon us, we can accomplish whatsoever we set our hearts, minds, and diligent efforts towards achieving.

Philippians 4:13: "I CAN do all things through Christ who Strengthens men."

I Can

There's a message I must tell myself
It's essential that it comes from me
That the dreams and goals I carry inside
God has granted the ability

When my enemies attempt to hinder my faith
Planting doubts to weaken my hands
It's up to me to remind my soul
That through Jesus Christ *I Can*

If He wills that I face some fiery trials
Or that I take an unpopular stand
If He calls me to a most challenging task
I must answer by saying *I Can*

See, the Lord, He is the source of my strength
He inspires my visions and plans
And because He births them in my heart
I must courageously say *I Can*

I Can is what I must keep preaching
Regardless of what others may say
Since these lofty dreams derived from God
I'm most certain He'll prosper my way

No spiritual forces can stop me
Nor any weapons formed by man
My only real threat is within me
It's ceasing to say that *I Can*

I can do all things through Jesus Christ
Yes, the sky is my limit, you see
I Can, I Can, Oh yes, I Can
That's the message I'm preaching to me!

I Am Unique

One of the most difficult things to grasp is one's sense of personal worth or uniqueness. It is so easy to recognize the talented traits in others while at the same time overlooking the unique gifts and talents that God has bestowed upon us. No one else ever has or ever will be exactly like us, nor can they be or do things in the manner in which God has specifically designed and assigned us to do. This poem aims to remind each of us that we are *UNIQUE* in God's eyes. It is not beneficial to us to spend our lives wishing we were like someone else or even longing to be anyone other than ourselves. We must search deeply within ourselves to discover the unique attributes and gifts that God has conferred upon us. Once we begin to discover our uniqueness, we must apply ourselves to cultivating every gift to its fullest potential, then humbly celebrate and appreciate who He has crafted us to be.

Psalm 139:14: "I Praise You because I'm Awesomely and Wonderfully made."

I Am Unique

I realize I'm *awesomely* and *wonderfully* made
I'm uniquely created to do great things
Yes, I'm *awesomely* and *wonderfully* made
I'll show you just what I mean!

There's no one else on this planet like me
I'm *designed* by the Master's hand
Yes, He crafted me, and *I'm so unique*
That He gave me my own plan!

No one else can be quite like me
See, I just can't be duplicated
No need to try; I'll tell you why
It's for something special I was created

Don't get me wrong, not trying to boast
Being boastful I would not dare
It's just my message to me, that when others I see
There's no need for me to compare!

Comparing is the trick of the enemy
To lead me into insecurity
And when my confidence springs a leak
I start questioning if I'm *Unique*

This message I speak is not just for me
God also wants each of you to see
That He Skilfully crafted your frame
And He carefully picked out your name

My dear friend, remember you're *awesome*
So never think that you're incomplete
Hold your head of up high, always reply
"I'm blessed, for I Am Unique!"

No Time to Waste

How often are we tempted to put off necessary tasks, the pursuit of dreams, or the rendering of deeds of kindness until a later date? We sadly assume that tomorrow is guaranteed to present us with another opportunity to undertake the tasks that we should prioritize today. This poem serves to remind us that our lives are short and that future opportunities are never certain; therefore, each day gifted to us by God must be utilized to its fullest. Life constantly changes; opportunities, skills, health, and even people that are present today may be gone tomorrow. Now is the time to invest ourselves fully into every worthwhile endeavour that is being stirred in our hearts by the Holy Spirit!

James 4:14: "What is your life? You are just a vapor that appears for a little while, then vanishes away."

No Time to Waste

Life has hit me with a harsh reality
That I won't be here always
There's a clock that won't stop ticking
And it's constantly shortening my days

This fact just can't be ignored
That there's simply *No Time to Waste*
If I'm to bring my Lord His glory
I must get moving right now with haste

See, time is not a luxury
It never pauses or stands still
So it's imperative that I work diligently
If I'm to fulfil my Master's will

Can't waste my time chasing life's pleasures
'Cause in the end, they're simply in vain
Instead I'll work on Heaven's agenda
To hear *Well Done*—that is my aim

So in the meantime I must get going
Use every gift God's given to me
'Jesus said the night is coming
When all my works shall suddenly cease

My yesterdays, they've all fled
And tomorrow's no guarantee
My today is all that I have
So the Lord gets the best of me

Because the clock just won't stop ticking
It is wise to pick up my pace
I can't afford to keep on delaying
I must run hard and finish my race!

MY NAME'S BEEN CHANGED

After making what appears to be catastrophic mistakes in life, so many of us often wonder if we can start over again. We wonder if it's even possible to recover from such regrettable and often shameful repercussions. *Thankfully, we have a Saviour, who is rich in grace, one who is willing to take on the humiliations of our lives and offer us a future glory that outshines the darkness or our pasts.* Through this poem I hope to inspire those who have felt that the horrendous mistakes of their past have disqualified them from experiencing a glorious future destiny, one in which Christ's reshapes their lives, transforming them into a person of profound usefulness and admiration!

Genesis 32:28: "Your NAME will no longer be Jacob, the man told him. From NOW ON you will be CALLED Israel."

My Name's Been Changed

I have stumbled, and I have fallen
Now left with scars and lots of shame
Starting to look like my life is over
'Cause I've utterly ruined my good name

I didn't see it at the time
How badly this road would surely end
Is there such a thing as second chances?
Can I possibly begin again?

The horrible things that I have done
They left me branded with a label
To even shake such disgrace
I didn't believe that I would be able

Then I heard the voice of Jesus
Saying, "I died for this very shame
I can wash you white as snow
I can provide a brand-new name

"I don't know if you have heard
But I specialize in tragic stories
If you'll be Mine and give Me time
You'll have a *new name* that's full of glory

"Dear child, you're not My first
And you certainly won't be My last
They'll be other broken lives
Who'll need rescuing from their pasts"

So as you walk in your new season
Be sure to tell about your story
Your shameful name it has been *changed*
And to God Be All the Glory

Get Back Up

Like so many, I find myself occasionally falling short of measuring up to the perfect godly standards of my Lord Jesus Christ. Though I sincerely strive to measure up to His call to be holy, there are times when the presence of sin remaining in my members causes me to stumble and miss His perfect mark. Like many genuine Christians who occasionally stumble in their walk of faith, my heart is broken by my failures, and at times I wander if I've exhausted my allotment of God's grace. But the Holy Spirit gently reminds me that He knows my frame, that I am flesh and therefore my journey is not about flawlessness but rather about a relentless pursuit of His holiness. In these stumbling moments, He freely imparts more grace, which enables me to *Get Back Up* from my stumbles and continue my journey towards sanctification and true holiness. Hence, this poem seeks to inspire those who are fearful that their stumbles have disqualified them from maximizing their godly potential and from fulfilling their God-ordained destinies. The message is simple: you can *Get Back Up Again!*

Proverbs 24:16: "For though a righteous man FALLETH seven times, He will GET UP again."

Get Back Up

Oh how so disappointing it is
To say "Father, I have sinned"
Lord, it's tearing me up inside
To be back in this place again

I know that we all fall short of Your glory
Yet that brings no comfort to me
Standing in this guilt and shame
It's the last place I want to be

Tell me how do I break this cycle
And conquer my stumbling ways
Will I ever overcome my weaknesses
And live Victorious all my days?

My heart desires so much to honour You
And never ever to bring You shame
To walk ever so purely before You
Bringing all honour unto Your name

Lord, how long must I continue wait
Before I receive my body of glory?
How my soul is longing for the day
When stumbling's no longer a part of my story

But In the meantime I'll keep on fighting
To win this battle against evil and sin
And if by chance I happen to stumble
I'll Get Back Up and Fight Again!

Heal Me

There are so many people carrying deeply embedded scars and secret struggles that they desperately long to break free from. In so many Christian circles, many don't feel at liberty to express these lingering issues openly for fear of being judged or even being shunned by fellow Christians. In such environments, though born-again, some are yet experiencing defeats in their private lives and are void of the steady flow of inner peace and joy that are promised as by-products of a born-again experience. This absence of true inner peace and joyfulness is due to the realization that they are still ensnared with past hurts, disappointments, and embarrassing private struggles. This poem was inspired on behalf of those who recognize that there are still levels of inner healing that need to take place in the innermost places of their hearts, to remind them that Jesus invites them to openly confess such struggles and to seek total healing at His hands!

Matthew 15:30: "Great crowds came to Him, and He HEALED THEM ALL."

Heal Me

Is there no balm in Gilead?
Asked one of the prophets of old
Tell me, is there someone available
To Heal the pain down in my soul?

Heaven sent us a *Great Physician*
Who had healing in His wings
He cured all manners of diseases
Even removed death's powerful sting!

As He walked the streets of Jerusalem
Blinded eyes began to see
People started coming from all around
Each one crying *"Lord Heal Me"*

The Bible contains such marvellous accounts
Of how broken lives were truly made whole
How many found strength for their weaknesses
And total deliverance for their souls

Like so many, I have been wounded
Countless times I've been let down
I'm trying so hard to keep on moving
While deep down inside I still feel bound

Send Your Word into my heart
And comfort my ailing soul
Total healing is what I'm pleading
Touch me now and make me *whole*

So with this prayer I do confess
I have no choice but to keep it real
Even though I've made some progress
Still got wounds that must be *Healed!*

Transparency (Show Your Wounds)

How many times have we secretly struggled with sins, weaknesses, and personal failings that we really wanted to reveal but didn't feel confident that others would still respect our profession of faith? It is in these shadows of secrecy that Satan wages his most effective warfare against Christians, holding them bound far too long in struggles that they could have been liberated from if only they felt the safety of being *Transparent* with other fellow Christians. This poem encourages believers to show and share our wounds, our struggles, and even our setbacks with other trustworthy mature-minded Christians. It is impossible to pray effectively for one another, as well as offer support and encouragement, when we are ignorant to each other's challenges. By being *Transparent,* those who are currently embroiled in private struggles can find solace in knowing that they are not alone in their battles against sin, the world, and the devil.

St. John 20:20: *"After He said this, He SHOWED them His hands and His sides."*

Transparency

How I wish that I could boast
That I've never stumbled or fell
When it comes to falling short
That I had no story to tell

But to other stumbling Christians
I'd be no source of help
'I'd have no point of reference
To aid their stumbling steps

Like Jesus, it is essential
To reveal my scars and wounds
It's the only means I have
To help the fallen in the room

See God's house is filled with people
Who are *destined* to have a *fall*
Even those who are sincerely striving
To measure up to His holy call

To restore my fellow Christians
There is but one necessity
If I'm to truly be able to help them
It requires *Transparency*

My failing steps I'm willing to tell
And my struggles I will not hide
It is impossible to help the fallen
If I'm hiding behind my pride

I'm not boasting about my weaknesses
Hear me now with clarity
Just want you to see the depth of His Grace
Through my own Transparency

Keep Calling

Every Christian will experience some moments when it appears that all their efforts in prayer are just not producing any desired outcomes. In all honesty, frustration with prayer and its seemingly slow results begin to gradually eat away our faith in the same manner in which termites slowly eat away at the walls of a home. Regardless of what appears as inactivity from Heaven, we are encouraged and better yet commanded by Jesus to be relentless in prayer. The message of this poem is to inspire persistence in prayer, to remind every Christian that those who remain diligent in prayer are the ones who reap its reward.

I Thessalonians 5:16–17: "Rejoice always. Pray without ceasing."

Keep Calling

What do you do when you've been praying
Yet it seems it's all in vain
What do you do when you see no remedy
For all your heartaches and pain

What do you do when you've been waiting
And not one thing has turned around
When you've been pressing and confessing
Still no breakthrough has been found

Yet the Bible is quite emphatic
That you must knock and knock again
Giving up just isn't an option
It takes persistence for you to win

Lord, are You telling me to *Keep Calling*
Even though nothing has seemed to change
Are You telling me all my persistence
In the end, won't be in vain

That's exactly what I'm saying
It's what My Word says to do
That if you just keep on knocking
I'm certain to open that door for you

My dear friend, you *Keep On Calling*
You stay right on those bended knees
In His appointed time, He'll answer
He's already heard your earnest pleas!

Just a Word from You

We all have moments when we feel overwhelmed by complexing circumstances in our lives. During such times, our emotions can become so unstable that leaning upon them can prove to be very unwise. It is extremely difficult, if not impossible, to make rational decisions during times of emotional duress. When encountering similar moments, I have found myself desperately in need of a timely, sound, and relevant Word from the Lord to keep me grounded and rational enough to make wise decisions. *A fresh Word from God is critical to seeing life's temporary adversities from God's eternal perspective.* The message of this poem is to inspire all to seek God's counsel and to await His directives when finding themselves at one of life's critical crossroads.

Jeremiah 37:17: "Is there a WORD from the Lord?"

Just a Word from You

Caught in the complexing storms of life
Seldom knowing what to do
Feeling like I'm losing my mind
Lord, I need a timely Word from You

A Word from You restores my hopes
And always gives order to my steps
It reminds me I'm not alone
That You are my present Help

A Word from You, always strengthens me
When my path gets rocky and rough
A Word from You carries me through
Whenever I feel like giving up!

Lord, just one fresh Word is what I need
'Cause I'm weary, weak, and worn
Only Your Word can anchor me
While I'm riding through this storm

Your Wonderful Word, yes, it is life
It gives nourishment to my soul
The weight of this world has broken me
Send me a Word that makes me whole!

Just *A Word*, one timely Word
Is what I need, I have no doubt
It's strong enough to break all chains
One Word from You will bring me out!

So as I wander through life's wilderness
Cause fresh *Manna* to fall from above
May it remind me of Your faithfulness
And reassure me of Your Love

Hold On—Change
Is Coming

I think that one of the hardest aspect of maturing as a Christian is learning how to wait and developing the ability to persevere joyfully, to labour faithfully, and to maintain enthusiastic worship all while waiting for change to occur in situations that are severely testing the very core of your faith. How do you keep the faith when none of your agonizing circumstances seem to be changing? In essence, how do you keep holding on to things, people, situations, and places when every ounce of human reasoning is screaming *Let Go? The inspirational message of this poem centres on reminding us that though change often moves slowly, it is certain to come in God's perfect timing and in His own uniquely crafted way!*

Job 14:14: "All the days of my appointed time, I will wait till MY CHANGE COMES."

Hold On—Change Is Coming

There are times we all feel like giving up
'Cause our way just seems too hard
We search around in every direction
And still can't find the Lord

We look to the right and then the left
Often wondering where He is
So we try to fix things by ourselves
Though His Word has said *Be Still!*

Remember, weeping may endure for a night
But in the morning we'll see the sun
It's the blessed assurance we have
That *Change* is going to *Come*

We should have learned from previous storms
That God will never let us down
No matter the wait, just keep the faith
Cause this too He'll turn around

The pace of change is always slow
But *Change i*s headed your way
So just hold on; change won't be long
God's bringing a brighter day

Stay encouraged, my blessed friend
Don't you worry, fear, or doubt
Our God's too Great, and He won't be late
He'll show up soon to bring you out!

His Bread Is Always Fresh

Often times we treat reading the Bible more as a task to be performed rather than a joyful time of communing with God. If we could change our perception of the Word of God and see it for what it really is, I believe we would look forward to incorporating it into our daily itineraries with joy. God's Word is food. It's literally the soul's bread or source of nourishment; it is always fresh or timely for every situation or season in our lives. This poem seeks to rekindle our passion and appreciation for reading the Scriptures. *It reminds us that God has a fresh loaf of encouragement, instruction, and correction ready to impart into our hearts and minds daily!*

Matthew 6:11: "Give us this day our DAILY BREAD."

His Bread Is Always Fresh

Lord, each day brings fresh issues
Battles always raging inside of my head
They leave me starving for Your guidance
I need a slice of Your Fresh Bread!

As my Shepherd, You gave me a promise
A luscious table You'd always spread
I'm coming now with desperate hunger
For my ration of Daily Bread

O Bread of Heaven, will You feed me
I'm at Your table, ready to eat
If I'm able to feast of Your Bread
All these struggles I'll surely defeat

Your Word is my *Fresh Manna*
Oh so Fresh, and it tastes so sweet
One daily slice does lighten my path
Your Bread is a lamp to my feet

With each dawning day, I'll keep coming
Into Your Presence to find sweet rest
It's at Your Table my faith is renewed
Cause Your Bread is Always So Fresh!

GOD'S GOT YOU

Our natural response to the vicissitudes of life is to become anxious and unsettled concerning our ability to survive such unexpected downturns. Life has a unique way of rattling our sense of security by throwing things into a state of utter chaos. When people, places, or situations that we deemed stable begin to destabilize, panic often rushes to the forefronts of our minds. It is in such moments of uncertainty that we need to be reminded that God is fully aware of the dilemmas surrounding us and that He has proactively set provisions in place to see us through! The inspiration behind this poem serves to quiet our anxieties by reminding every believer that *God's Got Us.* We are not experiencing trials that have somehow caught God unaware. *He has divinely positioned all the grace, support, and resources in place to sustain us in this season.*

Psalm 3:3: "But thou O LORD, art a shield for me, my glory, and the LIFTER UP of mine head."

God's Got You

Day upon day the pressure's building
Got me wondering if I'll make it through
Yet I hear this soothing voice
Saying, "Don't You Worry, *God's Got You!*"

I know you're fearful of the unknown
Wondering where these trials are going to end
Just remember yesterday's victories
And rest assured you'll be winning again!

See, God is our refuge and shield
Ever present in the moments we dread
His favour shall soon be revealed
For He's the *Lifter of our heads*!

It's in these seasons of uncertainty
Where the enemy plays on our fear
Trying to convince us we're in it alone
But rest assured, God's standing here!

Though His provisions are not always visible
Don't be alarmed by what you can't see
By faith you just keep on walking
And say to yourself, God's Got Me!

You're Not Alone

Despondency is a terrible state of mind that occasionally overcomes believers. We find ourselves facing intimidating issues that linger over us with a sense of invincibility. In such moments, we wonder if we are left to deal with such daunting situations alone, as if God has abandoned us to circumstances by which we are incapable of managing. It is while facing such moments of feeling helpless and alone that Satan wars against our faith. Our sense of uncertainty makes us vulnerable to his distortions of the facts, which cause us to question the faithfulness of our God. *The message of this poem it to restore our confidence that regardless of our frightful circumstances, we are never left to face them alone.* Jesus promises to be with us always, and with His presence besides us, we will emerge victorious!

Hebrews 13:5: "For he hath said, I will NEVER LEAVE thee, nor FORSAKE thee."

You're Not Alone

Troubles of life they often confound us
There are times things go so wrong
In the back of our minds we wonder
Am I facing these challenges alone?

Like Job, we search so desperately
For some sign that God's still here
Just hoping He'll utter a gentle whisper
Reassuring us that He's standing so near!

The Lord left a promise to Never Leave Us
That He'll always be right by our sides
Even in life's treacherous valleys
There He promised our steps to guide

I may move my presence to the sidelines
But never think that I've left the field
I know Satan's tempting you to doubt Me
I strongly encourage you not to yield!

My dear child, you're not alone
Though it might seem that way to you
I only ask that you will trust Me
Don't I always see you through?
I'll never ever leave or forsake you
'Cause to my heart you are so dear
You must remember when you can't see Me
That doesn't mean that I'm not near!

You Have Something to Live For

For many, life can seem very bleak at times. Faced with constant frustrations, disappointments, and emotional pain, they find themselves often wanting to give up. The scriptures teach that the absence of hope makes the heart sick; therefore, the remedy for such emotional sickness is the restoration of hope. This poem is a reminder that God has designed a good purpose for every life. No matter how bleak the circumstances, He has a desire to restore order and bring fulfilment to everyone who will place their trust in Him. It is God who declares, "Behold, I create all things new." *He is the God of new beginnings, and He has a new and better chapter for your life that's truly worth Living For!*

Ezekiel 16:6: "When I passed by you and saw you squirming in your blood, I said to you while you were in your blood, 'LIVE.' Yes, I said to you while you were in your blood, 'LIVE.'"

You Have Something to Live For

Your way seems bleak right now
Like there's nothing else to give
But here's a fresh word from the Lord
He's commanding your soul to *Live*

The Lord is saying that He's not through
Achieving the plans He had in mind
Marvellous things He's spoken over you
Long before the beginning of time!

Before the Master created this world
You were lingering in His thoughts
Like a Potter who shapes the clay
Your perfection He's going to wrought

This stormy season can seem so bleak
May even seem more peaceful to die
The Holy Spirit is saying Live On
I'm here to tell you the reason why!

There's an awesome purpose inside of you
One the devil doesn't want revealed
He's working hard to crush your faith
It's your great destiny he's trying to kill!

So keep telling yourself *I Must Live*
No matter how dreary things may get
Here's a timely Word from God
You ain't seen your best days YET!

More Precious than a Lily

As Christians we are clearly instructed by the Scriptures not to worry, yet worrying is something that we all are guilty of at one time or another. Life hurls so many challenging situations our way, problems that appear to have no immediate solutions to them. It is in such moments when we feel powerless to resolve these challenges that worry instinctively kicks in. We worry about providing for our families, if our health will endure, or if it can be recovered. We worry about employment opportunities or if our current jobs will endure. Life presents us with so many uncertainties that cause anxiety to grip our hearts. *This poem offers God's simple remedy to quiet our concerns. He points us to the glory of the LILY to remind us that if He so graciously cared for it, how much more would He care for us?*

Matthew 6:28, 30: "So why do you worry about clothing? Consider the LILIES of the field, how they grow, they neither toil nor spin . . . Wherefore, if God so clothe the grass of the field, which today is, and tomorrow is cast into the oven, shall he not much more clothe you, O ye of little faith?"

More Precious than a Lily

God told me not to worry
But my spirit is crying, *"Really?"*
Then He said, "Have you forgotten
My Revelation concerning the *Lily?*

"The Lily is truly gorgeous
A classic work of My creative hand
Though it's dressed in a splendid glory
Yet in the grass is where it stands

"It did not labour for all its beauty
The Lily received it all by grace
Yet I shaped it with careful precision
Though its glory is fading with haste

"If I could carefully dress a mere flower
Whose days will last just a few
Shouldn't that tell you, My dear child
I have provisions in store for you!"

Now don't you let your heart be troubled
Nor let these ole worries ruin your day
Just remember the *Lily's* sheer beauty
And know that God has a made away!

You and I are more precious than the *Lily*
That's the message our Saviour did tell
Let us quiet these worried thoughts
By saying to our souls that *"It is Well"*

God Makes a
Mean Gumbo

In this present world, we are presented with a plethora of experiences that range from times of celebrations to times of personal challenge, such as heartaches, disappointments, and even tragic disasters. Life simply presents us with such a mixture of experiences that it may appear at times that our emotions are riding a swift, twisting, bending roller coaster. When enduring such fluctuation of emotional highs and lows, it can be quite difficult trying to find purpose in all the perplexities we often endure. This poem highlights a unique southern cuisine that contains many differing ingredients that on the surface may not appear to complement one another, yet when masterfully combined together, it accomplishes a dish that is delightsome to the taste buds. *The poem's message references this delightful dish as an analogy of how God masterfully intertwines the extremely painful, disappointing, and challenging experiences of our lives and causes them to work together for our good!*

Romans 8:28: "And God causes all things to WORK TOGETHER for the good of them who love the Lord, to them that are the called according to His purpose."

God Makes a Mean Gumbo

Consider a Bowl of Gumbo
With all its tasteful parts
A combination of delectable ingredients
Warm and soothing to the heart

It's unique in how it's made
An assortment of many different things
Yet when *skilfully meshed* into the pot
What a delightful taste it brings

Then I thought about how my God
Who says all things work for good
With my challenges, He makes spiritual gumbo
In ways that only He could!

He takes all the things I've gone through
Test and trials, sunshine and rain
My ups and downs, smiles and frowns
He causes them all to bring me gain

A Master Chef in the kitchen of life
He takes my joys and miseries
And places them all in His pot
Then says, "Come taste and see

"How I took what you thought was bad
Masterfully used it for your good
Without a doubt, it all worked out
Exactly like I promised it would!"

When life's going crazy all around you
May you strive to stay meek and humble
Remember your God"s in Heaven's kitchen
He's Whipping up a Mean Gumbo!

Good Lessons
from Bad Times

It is a fact that many of us dread going through difficult times. If we had our way, we would only permit sunny days into our lives. But because God's thoughts and ways are higher than ours, He permits struggles, adversities, discomforts, and disruptions of all sorts because in them lie valuable revelations of His power, character, and faithfulness that bring greater perspective to our lives. We seldom delight in difficult circumstances, yet extremely valuable lessons are learned when we are forced to endure afflictions. *This poem discloses the value of our difficult times of testing, highlighting the wisdom and spiritual enlightenment that's gained from our so-called "Bad Times."*

Psalm 119:71: "It is GOOD for me that I have been AFFLICTED; that I might LEARN thy statues."

Good Lessons from Bad Times

There's an often-heard cliché
Where there's no pain, there is no gain
This explains why God sends trouble
Increasing my faith that is His aim

My adversities come to teach me
Beautiful lessons that shape my life
Wonderful truths I'd never know
If I never ever suffer strife!

My times of lack they came to teach me
That on God I have to lean
Not on jobs, people, or places
I learned that He alone is my Everything

My betrayals they came to teach me
That my faith can't lie in men
I learned that God's a present Help
Who sticks by me through thick and thin!

It was Good to have been afflicted
I learned that troubles don't last always
That if I keep my eyes on Jesus
He'll be the Light that brightens my day

Its the bad times that have taught me
How to keep on keeping on
That my *battles* are already *over*
And my *victories* are already *won!*

There's a Blessing in the Pressing

In each of our lives, there arise moments when we feel like giving into weariness and frustration. The path in front of us seems cluttered with too much debris. In such moments, we find it difficult to continue to push forward due to the absence of any indication that our current predicaments are improving. It is in these trying moments that we can choose either to bow out or to press forward with the belief that our perseverance will yield a positive outcome. *This poem reminds us that a blessing awaits us if we opt to keep pressing towards the goals and dreams that our faith in God has given birth to!*

Philippians 3:14: "I PRESS toward the mark for the prize of the high calling of God in Christ Jesus."

There's a Blessing in the Pressing

They say there's a *Blessing in the Pressing*
And this, I believe, is true
But let me be the first to admit
That Pressing ain't easy to do!

'Cause life's struggles, tests, and trials
They just keep on coming my way
At times it seems so challenging
Just to bend my knees to pray!

I've heard the wonderful sermons
Telling me I've got to fight on
That if I keep on pushing forward
I'd see that the battle's already won!

Please Tell me, how do I press
Towards the mark I can no longer see?
Please Tell me how to keep the faith
Amid so much grief and misery!

But suddenly I hear *His* voice
Saying, "Gaze your eyes upon *Me*
I've never failed you or forsaken you
Pressing is the key to your victory!

"If you press on a little further
No matter how hard the testing!
I'm your God who cannot lie
There's a Blessing in your Pressing!"

So to all my weary siblings
Don't you ever give up this fight
'Cause we got that blessed assurance
That everything's going to be all right!

There's a Blessing in the Pressing
So Press into your Best!

LIVING RIGHT DOES PAY OFF

Psalm 73 provides an account of the transparent testimony of Asaph. Though he has spent the bulk of his life in the service of the Lord, he found himself having a momentary crisis of faith. Having observed what appeared to be a great injustice as it pertained to the prosperity of wicked men, Asaph found himself wondering if *Living Right* really pays off. Sometimes it can appear that those who violate godly principles, who seek to serve their own agendas, are some of the most materially prosperous people in the world. In contrast, there are many who sincerely serve the Kingdom of God faithfully and sacrificially, yet they endure a very meager existence, often getting by with the bare necessities of life. This poem serves to remind the faithful servants of Christ that God honours those who strive to live for His glory and whether it be in this present life or the next, *Living Right Will Pay Off!!*

I Corinthians 15:58: "Therefore, my beloved brethren, be ye steadfast, unmoveable, always abounding in the work of the Lord, for your LABOR IS NOT IN VAIN."

Living Right Does Pay Off

Does living right pay off?
We wonder when things get hard
Yet this question often arises
When we see no movement from God

When we look around the world
And watch evildoers advance!
Living life to the grandest degree
Yes, they sing, they laugh, they dance!

Yet sometimes we the godly
Are often burdened and bogged down!
We're stressed, vexed, and irritated
With little smiles and lots of frowns!

We wonder how this can be
That the ungodly seem at rest!
That many who are acting the worst
Seem to be the ones enjoying the best

Will living right reward me?
Yes! That's what the scripture says
Take a look at King Hezekiah
Living right prolonged his days

When sick and close to death
He prayed, "Lord, remember my walk
I've lived faithfully for Your glory

Lord, my life was more than talk!"

Upon review of his godly résumé!
The Lord had a change of mind
"Oh King, because you've lived right
I'll grant you a little more time!"

Yes, living right pays off!
So, saints, keep doing your thing
Don't you listen to that ole devil
You keep striving to please your King

The Devil Is a Liar

As Christians, the spiritual battles that we fight are waged deep within our minds. It is there that Satan seeks to manipulate how we perceive life's challenges. Satan's primary tactic is to produce arguments against the truths of God's Word; these arguments are often based on current conditions and circumstances in our lives that seem to contradict the very assurances that we have received from the Holy Scriptures. *The message of this poem reminds us that Satan's presentation of the facts is always a distortion of the realities of glorious purposes that God is working to accomplish in our lives.* He is a *Liar*, and we must never forget it!

St. John 8:44: "Ye belong to your father, the devil . . . for he's the father of lies."

The Devil Is a Liar

The devil's a notorious Liar
So let me show you why
He's a scheming, sneaky crook
That's always on the pry!

See, he has no real power
Shenanigans are his trade
He convinces us to doubt
All the ways that God has made

He takes God's simple truth
Then turns it all around
Working hard to shake our faith
Till our hopes come tumbling down!

The devil tells you that you won't make it
That God won't see you through!
So cease your prayers and your praises
'Cause they just ain't working for you!

Now my question to all the saints
Whose report will you believe?
The faithful Word of a Loving God
Or that murderous *lying thief*!

Yes, the devil, he is a Liar
'Even Jesus says it's so
And when he told his lies to our Saviour
Jesus told him where to go!

Satan, get you and your lies behind me
I refuse to give you space
I will trust in my Saviour's power
Ever clinging His grace!

Yes, ole Devil you're a liar
The Holy Scriptures make it clear
And now that you have been exposed
We have nothing else to fear!

A Love I Can't Explain

One thing I still find difficult to truly comprehend is the unconditional love of God. Just surveying my own life, when I consider the dark history of my past, coupled with the imperfections of my present walk, there are simply times where I struggle with the concept of being totally forgiven and fully accepted as beloved. There are times I've wondered if I had possibly exhausted God's grace towards me or depleted my share of His mercy. It is in such moments that the Holy Spirit reminds me that I am loved with an everlasting love, that God has already demonstrated the boundless depth of His love towards me when He sent His only begotten Son to die for my sins. *In view of such magnanimous love, I am left in awe. Herein lies the meaning and inspiration behind this poem!*

1 John 3:1: "Behold WHAT MANNER OF LOVE the Father has bestowed upon us that we should be called the children of God."

A Love I Can't Explain

Wow! Muggers, rapists, and robbers,
Yes, people who've caused others pain,
Even they are offered forgiveness.
It's a love I can't explain!

For Sinners caught up in madness,
Some with deeds too shameful to tell,
Yet for them, He shed His blood,
Saving many from the gates of Hell.

As I look over my life with wonder,
At the dark, twisted things I've done,
Can't grasp why You chose to love me,
Why You're not ashamed to call me Your son!

Such a love I find mysterious,
'Cause my flaws still cause You pain!
But even then, You hold me closely.
This kind of love I can't explain!

You're so patient with all my stumbling.
My weaknesses You steadily bear.
In my most disheartening moments,
You faithfully show me that You care!

So as I gaze at the Cross, dear Jesus,
At the unconditional love You displayed!
Your tender mercies leave me speechless,
And at Your grace, I stand amazed!

JUST STAY CLOSE

Take a moment and consider the nature as well as the physical attributes of sheep. This mildly natured creature is laden with unimpressive traits that leave it vulnerable to decimating attacks from ruthless predators. Sheep have poor eyesight, so they can't identify threats from afar; they have flabby frames that lack muscular stamina and speed, so sheep can't fight off or outrun their attackers. Such lack of physical prowess makes their chances of survival seem low. The sheep's only defence is to *Stay Close* to their shepherd, who is wise and skilled at providing for and protecting them. This poem serves to remind every Christian that we are the sheep of God's fold. *Our survival against the wiles of the devil is solely contingent on our willingness to Stay Close to our Shepherd, the Lord Jesus Christ.*

Psalm 23:4: "Yea though I walk through the valley of death, I will fear no evil, for THOU ART WITH ME."

Just Stay Close

Yes, the Lord, He is my Shepherd,
But where He leads I don't always like!
Some of these scary paths He chooses
Often leave my soul affright!

Right when it seems my path is smooth,
He suddenly changes the terrain!
Now we're on a path so rugged
It leaves bruises, scars, and pain!

I scream, "Lord, where are you taking me?"
It feels like the valley of death.
He says, "We're staying on this path
Till not one of your fears are left!

"I thought you said you trusted Me,
That your life was Mine's to hold.
I know which paths to lead you on,
To shape your faith into solid gold.

"All I need is that you Stay Close,
Just don't stray too far from me.
As your Shepherd, I will protect you
From all your enemies!

"You *Stay Closely* near my bosom,
Let not fear cause you to roam.
No matter how scary the valley,
I promise to get you home!"

Yes, the Lord, He is my Shepherd,
But I still have much to learn.
That's why He keeps on leading me,
Through these stressful twists and turns!

Dear Shepherd, I'll continue to follow.
And in my strength I'll never boast.
I know the key to my survival
Is just simply Staying Close!

THY KINGDOM COME

As the perils of this present world are mounting before us, there is an ever-increasing longing for peace, prosperity, and security among the inhabitants of this earth. Sadly, mankind doesn't seem to grasp the realization that no matter how noble our pursuit of universal peace and prosperity may be, it can't and never will be accomplished through human efforts. (All our treaties, global alliances, and economic summits are doomed to fail at the end of the day.) This long-desired thirst for universal blessing will only be realized at the appearing of our Lord Jesus Christ, who shall establish an *Everlasting Kingdom* flowing with uninterrupted peace and prosperity. This is essentially why this poem is a reminder for us to sincerely pray with all earnestness, *"Thy Kingdom Come."*

Matthew 6:10: "THY KINGDOM COME, thy will be done in the earth as it is in heaven."

Thy Kingdom Come

Lord, we're searching ever so desperately
For lasting peace to quiet these storms,
But such a peace we'll never experience,
Not Until Thy Kingdom Comes!

You're the promised Sun of Righteousness,
And at *Your Coming* You will bring
Everlasting Peace and Joyfulness,
For You'll have *Healing in Your Wings!*

See, the wisdom of man is faulty.
All their treaties are doomed to fail.
Our Curse is just too strong!
King of Kings, You must prevail!

The Prophets of Old have faithfully declared
That You're coming back again
To restore the earth from this horrible curse
By ridding it of all this Sin!

Yes, Our sinful heart's the real Issue.
It's the source of all our ills.
Our troubles, they're self-inflicted.
If only we could do Your will!

May we bow our hearts before You,
Ever praying Thy Will be done,
Knowing things will not get better,
No, Not Until Thy Kingdom Comes!

Even so, come, Lord Jesus,
And all the Blessings of Heaven Bring!
For the saints of all the ages
Are waiting anxiously for our King!

HE'S COMING SOON

Many of our modern-day sceptics who hold a cynical view of Christianity often attempt to discredit the second coming of Jesus Christ by focusing on the fact that the prophecy concerning His appearance is now over two thousand years old. To some the prophecy simply serves as a myth to a weak and hapless segment of people who lack the courage to face the challenges of this life. *This poem serves as a reminder to the believers to keep our expectations high concerning our Lord's appearance. It is also a strong warning to the sceptics that His arrival is sure to come, and what a horrifying day it will be for those unprepared for such a sudden, glorious, and shocking appearance!*

Revelation 1:7: "Behold, he COMETH with the clouds; and every eye shall see him."

He's Coming Soon

It'll be a *Day* like no other
Every eye gazing with a stare
The True King has made His arrival
His Blazing Glory now fills the air!

All His saints riding beside Him
On white horses they cover the sky
Powerful sounds of trumpets now blaring
All the Angels with glory, they fly!

While the saints rejoice at His Presence
Every sinner is shaking with fear
Lacking faith, they doubted His coming
To their shock He suddenly appears!

Now the King has come with power
His enemies are starting to quake
The mighty men are now running for shelter
All the demons have started to shake!

Many never believed it would happen
Yet this *Day* has come to light
The masses caught unprepared
Are now facing an awful plight!

The hour of judgement has finally come
It's the message His prophets did tell
Now lack of faith and genuine repentance
Has their souls now destined for Hell!

This situation could've been avoided
All was needed was just to believe
When His Grace was offered freely
They just simply had to receive!

Now the Lord is Soon to Come
Tell me, will you be caught off guard?
Why don't you take this precious moment
And accept Him Now as your Lord!

Portrait of a Blessed Man

Society deems a man to be blessed or successful by such vain standards as the accumulation of material wealth, positions of prestige and influence, as well as their academic achievements. *Though such accomplishments are noteworthy, it would behove every man to know how God defines a blessed man.* This poem brings to light God's depiction of the type of man in whom the Lord delights in and in whom He characterizes as *Blessed!* May the message of this poem inspire a generation of men to seek after the heart and will of God!

Psalm 1:1: "Blessed is the man that walketh not in the counsel of the ungodly . . . but his delight is in the law of the Lord, and in His law doth he meditate day and night."

Portrait of a Blessed Man

Blessed is the man who seeks after God,
Who walks with Him hand in hand.
Blessed is the man devoted to prayer,
Ever pursuing the Master's plan!

Blessed is the man who proudly proclaims,
That loving the Lord is very cool.
Yes, this man will prosper in life,
He will avoid becoming a fool!

See, the man who delights in the Lord,
Is much wiser than all the rest.
With God on his side, ever his guide,
This man is destined to be blessed!

God will bless his going out,
And bless when he comes back in.
God will faithfully fight his battles,
This man can't help but win!

This message I send to my brothers,
For God, you take your *Stand.*
Know that God is writing your story,
He's Calling you a *Blessed man!)*

BREAK THE MOULD

We are in an age where the pressure to conform to the ideologies of the liberal world is at an all-time high. Society is placing great demand on the Christian community to depart from its principles of godly conduct and morality. In this age that stresses inclusiveness and acceptance of all behavioural practices, many Christians have determined it to be more advantageous to conform to the values of the world than to resist its MOULDING. *This poem highlights the Christian's unique calling, which is to Break the Moulding of this ungodly world and instead be transformed (shaped) into the godly image of our Lord Jesus Christ!*

Romans 12:2–2: *"And be not CONFORMED [shaped] to this world: but be ye TRANSFORMED by the renewing of your mind."*

Break the Mould

I've been born into a world that's ruthless
That at times is selfish and cold
Yet I'm called not to conform to it
But rather to Break The Mould!

This world will often encourage me
To please myself at every turn
But I've put on the yoke of Christ
It's His ways I now must learn!

The prince of this world entices me
To set my heart on silver and gold
Jesus says to seek righteousness first
So again I must *Break The Mould!*

Breaking this mould won't make me popular
For not many are doing the same
But I'm called to a higher purpose
It's to bring glory to Jesus's name!

So I take up my cross to follow Christ
Freely surrendering my heart and soul
Praying each day to be more like Him
Thus striving to *Break The Mould!*

I present my body as a sacrifice
Now cleanse me through and through
Transform me by Your mighty hand
And *Shape me* to be more like You!

He Never Said It Would Be Easy

Serving in the work of the Lord is both rewarding and fulfilling; yet there are times when the challenges associated with His service can become painful, stressful, and often times met with thankless attitudes. In these trying seasons, the adversities can seem so much greater than the rewards, leaving many sincere and faithful servants conflicted about whether to continue to push forward in the Master's service or to bow out altogether. It's in such seasons that we must remember that no matter how meaningful the work of Ministry is, Jesus never said it would be easy! *This poem reminds us that persevering in the work of the Lord requires that we pray earnestly for divine grace to finish the good works that we have started.*

Matthew 25:39: "Going a little farther, He fell facedown and prayed, 'My Father, if it is possible, let this cup pass from Me. Yet not as I Will, but as You Will!'"

He Never Said It Would Be Easy

Doing good ain't always easy.
Matter of fact, it can be quite hard,
Especially in trying seasons,
When there's no sight or sound from God!

See, the task of serving others
At times becomes a strain.
They're so busy reaping your efforts
That they fail to see your pain!

So you pray for another option,
One that gives you some relief,
'Cause the agony of your mission
Is making you question your beliefs.

You're in your Garden of Gethsemane!
And it seems you're all alone.
You're crying ever so tensely
To be heard at Heaven's Throne!

Lord, can You make this a little easier?
You know how miserable I feel.
Can You please lighten this load
So I can finish doing Your will!

But Your Will's not meant to be easy!
That is why You termed it a Cross!
There's a crown that's sure to be rewarded
For those who are willing to pay the Cost!

As this way gets harder before me
And I'm tempted to cut and run,
Grant me the grace to endure
Until Your Will Is Done!

I'M NEVER LEAVING
YOUR HOUSE

The House of God serves such an important role in the lives of Christians. It is the place where Christian fellowship is renewed, where the hopes of Christians are rekindled, and where their souls are refreshed through inspirational worship of the Living God. Because it is the hub of Spiritual revitalization, Satan is always launching both subtle and vicious attacks to disrupt both the unity of the fellowship. *This poem serves to remind us to treasure the beautiful gift of Christian fellowship that takes place in the House of God! We mustn't allow the devil's efforts to diminish our joy of entering the courts of our God.*

Psalm 23:6: "Surely goodness and mercy will follow me all the days of my life, and I will DWELL in the HOUSE of the LORD FOREVER."

I'm Never Leaving Your House

There's no other place for me.
No, I'm never leaving Your House.
It's the place of my deliverance,
Where Your Word does bring me Out!

It's in Your House that praises ring,
Where the joy of the Lord abounds.
It's in Your House that my soul finds lifting
Every time life knocks me down!

In Your House there's spiritual healing
And Water for the thirsty soul.
Where the Bread of Life is served,
Where the broken are being made whole.

So, devil, you can try all you want
To push me from this place.
But I'm determined to dwell right here,
For this House contains my Grace!

There's only One thing I desire of Him.
And I'll seek it with all my heart,
That no matter what life throws my way,
I'm staying in the House of God!

You Made the Difference

Pure and passionate worship is often generated by a willingness to look back over the scope of our lives and reflect on how things could have turned out if God had not mercifully intervened on our behalf. Jesus said, "No man comes unto me except he is drawn by the Father's loving hand"; therefore, it is the Father's grace that is the determining factor between whether many of us become the latest tragic statistic, versus having the opportunity to live an abundant life. *This poem is designed to rekindle our appreciation and recognition of the riches of God's amazing grace that's been lavishly conferred upon us!*

Psalm 124:1: "If it had not been the Lord who was on our side."

You Made the Difference

As I'm looking back over my life
My heart does beam with pride
Just thinking how blessed I am
To have had You by my side!

It was You who Made The Difference
In the wonderful way my life's turned out
Your loving grace and tender mercies
Were the keys without a doubt!

I could have easily been a statistic
Another person with a tragic end
Yet You came along beside me
And You graciously took me in!

You brought Your light into my heart
With Your Spirit renewed my mind
You snatched me from the darkness
Yes, it was just in the nick of time!

Before Satan could fulfil his plan
To corruptly fill my heart
And lead me to my destruction
Before my destiny could ever start!

So as I'm reflecting upon Your goodness
The Difference is clear to me
Lord, If it had not been for You
There's just no telling where I would be!

Show Me Your Ways

God has declared, "My thoughts are not your thoughts. Neither are my ways your ways." This powerful statement reveals that God responds to circumstances in manners totally opposite to the way we as humans do. It is therefore incumbent that we diligently seek to know His heart and to accurately understand His revealed Word so that we can respond to situations and challenges His way and not in ours! *May this poem inspire each of us to diligently pursue a deeply intimate relationship with our Lord, one that allows Him to reveal His ways to us in order to transform us into His image!*

Psalm 103:7: "He made known HIS WAYS to Moses and His deeds to the children of Israel."

Show Me Your Ways

How can I get know You better?
How can I please You all my days?
My heart longs to bring You Glory,
If only I can know Your Ways!

Reveal Yourself to my seeking heart,
Cause my shallow mind to see
The wondrous grace that you display
For countless sinners such as me!

For you possess no respect of persons.
Even sinners receive your best.
For both the sinner and the righteous
Can testify that they've been blessed!

Show me how You're still so faithful
To those of us who make You frown!
How You keep giving second chances
When Your children keep falling down!

If I'm to handle these trials correctly,
Then in Your Presence I have to stay,
Humbly seeking, ever demanding,
That you Show Me All Your Ways!

Can't Fake It—The Pressure's Real

Society often frowns upon admissions of weaknesses. Somehow it seems that we are mandated to show a false sense of bravado at all times. Even in Christian circles, there can be a subtle pressure to profess that all is well, when in reality believers may be inwardly coming apart! It is this false pretence of strength that often leads to secret entanglements in the lives of Christians, who may have better served themselves by admitting that they were feeling the strain or vulnerabilities while facing challenging circumstances. *This poem highlights the fact that some of God's most accomplished servants encountered moments where their faith was stretched to its limits. We need to know that it's okay to admit to others when we're feeling overwhelmed by life's difficult challenges.*

2 Corinthians 1:8: "*For we would not, brethren, have you IGNORANT of our TROUBLE which came to us in Asia, that we were PRESSED OUT OF MEASURE, and ABOVE STRENGTH, insomuch that we DESPAIRED even of life.*"

Can't Fake It—the Pressure's Real

Just fake it till you make it,
But I can't keep faking this feeling,
'Cause the pressure within is mounting,
And it's got me sort a reeling!

Been saying I'm strong and holding on,
Doing my best to not sound weak.
But if the truth was to be told,
I'm being knocked right off my feet!

Life's been very tough lately.
It's getting hard to force a smile.
Thought this storm would be over by now,
But it's been holding for quite a while!

People ask me how I'm doing,
But they're just trying to be polite,
If I took the time to tell my story,
They'd be sitting with me all night!

See this trial's really testing me,
So my testimony, I just can't fake.
I'm being pressed beyond my strength,
And I think I'm about to break!

So when you see me still a pushing,
Don't just glance, or give a stare.
Drop me a word of sweet encouragement
And make sure to send a prayer!

Stand Down—It's Not Your Fight

We all are tempted to rise up and fight against all the perceived acts of injustice that we deem to be unfairly directed towards us! We want to exercise vengeance and see people pay for their callous acts of insensitivity and cruelty, yet Scripture teaches that our acts of human aggression never produce the righteousness of God. Clearly interpreted, God says that our attempts to straighten things out usually results in making matters worse! *The clear message of this poem serves to remind us that God can fight far more effectively for us on issues of cruelty and injustice than we could ever for ourselves.* As a matter of fact, He encourages us to Stand Down and let Him deal with things His way and in His own timing.

2 Chronicles 20:15: "Do not be afraid or discouraged . . . for the BATTLE is not yours, but God's."

Stand Down—It's Not Your Fight

How tempted are we to get even,
When others don't do us right!
This thought, it burns within us,
If only God would let me fight!

But the kind of fight that I would wage,
I'm certain it wouldn't be best!
Yes, by the time that I got finished,
My testimony would be a mess!

If I could just handle it my way,
I'd make my enemies pay the price!
I'd exhaust every possible option,
And not one of them would be nice!

But the wisest thing to do,
Is *Stand Down* and just be still!
Let the Lord fight the battle,
While I stay in the Master's will!

See, what I've come to recognize,
Is that the battle is just a story.
It's a God-ordained dilemma,
Designed for Him to get the glory!

So, my friend, if you are troubled,
Because others have done you wrong!
You give that battle over to Jesus,
And Victory will be your song!

MIND-BLOWER

The Bible reveals a God who is exceptional, extraordinary, marvellous, and all-powerful, yet all these superlatives do not give justice to His indescribable make-up. Simply put, He literally blows the mind when gazing upon the extraordinary feats that are recorded of Him in the Bible. This amazing God created all things from nothing, parted seas, rained bread from the sky, took the heat from the fire, opened blinded eyes, and raised men from the dead, just to name a few of His amazing feats. This same God commands us to pray always, believing that ALL THINGS are possible to them that believe! *This poem is designed to ignite an expectation in our hearts that we too can be recipients of mind-blowing acts of God's favour!*

Ephesians 3:20: "Now unto Him who is able to do exceedingly, abundantly above all that we ask or think."

The Mind-Blower

The God of the Bible is one of a Kind.
His awesome résumé simply blows the mind!
There's absolutely nothing He cannot do.
He's got a *mind-blowing* blessing in store for you!

He's healed the sick and gave sight to the blind.
He even raised the dead from time to time!
The Lepers He cleansed of dreadful disease.
Those tormented in mind, He set at ease!

This God has even parted the seas
And He told the Sun to stand still!
He even forced mighty demons
To bow to His Holy will!

By His power a donkey spoke.
And pure water was turned into wine!
He took the heat out of the fire.
Literally blowing the poor king's mind!

This Awesome God, answers our prayers.
With hands wide-open, embraces our cares!
All things are possible to those who believe
Mind-Blowing blessing, they're destined to receive!

CREATION IS PREACHING

The heavens declare the glory of the Lord, and the earth testifies to His handy work. It is amazing that with all the visible evidence of His extraordinary wisdom, power, and creative genius, foolish men still seek to disprove God's existence! God's presence and power are clearly seen through all that He has created, the exquisite beauty of nature, the awesome allure of the expanse of heaven, as well as the awesome and wondrous make-up of humankind—they all speak loudly of His existence, His supreme intellect, and His unlimited power! *This poem highlights the fact that the creation is preaching powerful messages to earth's inhabitants every day. The messages are simple: God Is Real, His Wisdom is to be sought, His greatness is to be adored, and His Sovereignty is to be recognized!*

Psalm 19:1: "The HEAVENS DECLARE the glory of God and the firmament shows forth His handy work."

Creation Is Preaching

The Creaton Preaches all around us
It delivers a powerful sermon each day
Through the moon and stars above us
Through that great Big Milky Way!

Through the beautiful flowers before us
Through the green and luscious trees
Through the birds that soar above us
And through those teeny, tiny little bees!

Creation declares there's A God
Its uniqueness tells the story
It speaks of all His wonder
Of His wisdom and His glory!

Who else out there could design
A universe that works so fine
With billions of spinning galaxies
So many, they blow your mind!

Then with one final look in the mirror
An awesome creature is revealed
It's a walking, talking man
Showing the world that God is Real!

Yes, the Heavens declare His glory
And all creation is telling His story
That He's God in Heaven above
And we all are so blessed to have His Love!

LET IT START WITH GOD

How many times have we started down roads or set our efforts towards accomplishing goals that in hindsight we can admit that we never took the time to consult with God on those matters? Oftentimes we run up against obstacles that we did not consider would become problems during the initial stages of our pursuits. Such unsuspecting dilemmas so often leave us frustrated, defeated, or clueless as to how to work our way through them. *This poem serves to remind us that in all our ways we should acknowledge God, seeking His guidance, assistance, blessing, support, and protection before we set out upon the adventurous yet unpredictable paths of life!*

Genesis 1:1: "In the BEGINNING GOD."

Let It Start with God

I just wonder if at the Beginning,
Circumstances would be as hard.
If before we made our moves,
We were sure to *Start With God!*

Can we agree that oftentimes,
When we leave Him at the end,
We find ourselves with much regret,
Often wondering what might have been!

If we had spent more time in prayer,
Before we made those hasty steps,
Or before we threw in the towel,
We waited patiently for His help!

If before we spoke a word,
We spoke with Him at first.
Many situations would get better
Instead of often getting worse!

If before we started building,
We made sure we had His hands,
What we built would not have crumbled
But would've stood as He had planned!

Friends, when God is our *Beginning,*
Our losing becomes *Winning!*
All our goals and dreams are blessed,
And at the *End,* we have sweet *Rest!*

If Only I Had Listened

The shocking truth about many of life's perils is that a large number of them could have been avoided if we had simply consulted with the Holy Scriptures to hear what God had to say about our life's choices. Not only does He disclose principles that lead to blessings, but the Lord also clearly detailed what practices lead to cursed conditions in our lives. Still, so many choose to flat out ignore what God has decreed and rush swiftly into their own set of heartaches and calamities. So many choose not hearken to the voice of parents, pastors, teachers, or well-informed associates who raised the red flags and offered warnings about impending doom if certain paths were followed. *This poem's aim is to highlight the importance of acknowledging and adhering to God's Word, it reminds us of the value of heeding the wise counsellors that God has graciously planted in our lives.*

Proverbs 5:7: "Now then, my sons, LISTEN to me and do not DEPART from the words of my mouth."

If Only I Had Listened

In a world overflowing with heartache,
I wonder how much could be avoided.
If many would simply *Listen*
To the Wisdom of God that's been recorded!

In His love, He recorded in scripture
Transcendent truths so rich with Life,
Yet so many have refused to Hearken,
Ending up in a world of Strife!

Tragedies and hardships self-inflicted,
Miserable burdens carried each day.
Many of them could've been avoided
By simply listening to what God had to say!

See, the enemy of our soul is crafty,
Always reminding us that we have a choice,
But the many options he presents
Never seem to contain God's voice!

That slick devil offers pleasures
But never discloses how they will end.
God's Word is shouting *Beware!*
There's danger lurking inside that sin!

"If only I had Listened,"
Says the poor soul who's now in pain,
Who wasted time with temporal pleasures,
Only to find that it was all in vain!

The wages of sin is *always death*,
So Listen closely to the voice of God.
Obedience will lead to blessings,
But the path of Sinners is Always Hard!

ALL WALLS SHALL FALL

Whenever we are moving in pursuit of God-inspired dreams, obstacles are destined to arise. These obstacles can appear so enormous that they leave us doubting the possibility of achieving our goals. *Like Joshua facing the Walls of Jericho, there will be walls standing in front of our dreams that must be conquered if we are to fulfil our God-given potential.* The enemy of our soul has built all types of walls in our lives—walls of insecurity, low self-confidence, fear of failure, lack of support, or the lack of visible resources. Yet if God has birthed dreams and goals in our hearts, *we can be assured that His grace is available to knock down every wall standing in front of destinies.* Through this poem it is my hope to inspire everyone who dares to dream to not allow those *Walls* to discourage you or dissuade you from pursuing what God has placed in your heart and mind.

Joshua 6:20: "So the people shouted, and the priests blew the trumpets, and when the people heard the sound of the trumpet, the people shouted with a great shout and the WALL FELL DOWN FLAT."

All Walls Shall Fall

To those with dreams that stand so tall
This poem is your summoning call
Pay your obstacles no attention
All those WALLS are about to FALL!

With God being on your side
None of those walls can ever stand
They can't block you from your dreams
Your destiny is in His hands!

It's not by your power or by your might
You must remember while you pursue
God's anointing shall bring it to pass
The dream's too great to rest on you!

So don't you keep staring at that *Wall*
Start shouting and giving God praise
The foundation is starting to crumble
It's Falling Down in a few more days!

You keep the faith, O faithful dreamer
Your obstacles march right around
God brought you to this great big wall
So you can watch Him bring it down!

Yes, those Walls that seem unconquerable
They may as well be made out of *Straw*
When the Lord is finished with them
He's gonna leave you standing in *Awe!*

FEET SO BEAUTIFUL

This poem is dedicated to my fellow labourers in this Gospel of Jesus Christ. Oftentimes it may feel as though our labours are often overlooked, that our roles are being diminished in society's view for a plethora of reasons. It appears that there are others (celebrities, athletes, businessman, etc.) whose work and labours are less influential in positively shaping society as a whole, yet they are more honoured, more celebrated, and oftentimes more appreciated by the masses. *Yet the Bible only identifies one classification of persons as having Beautiful Feet!* This description rests with the humble, genuine, yet often underappreciated servants who are called to preach the Good News of the Gospel of Jesus Christ. This poem reflects upon your unique beauty and is penned as a reminder to those whose souls have been saved and lives transformed by your labours, to pause, celebrate, and appreciate the *Beauty of Your Feet!*

Romans 10:15: "And how can anyone preach unless they are sent? As it is written: 'How BEAUTIFUL are the FEET of those who bring good news!'"

Feet Oh So Beautiful

In a generation that worships celebrities
Willing to dance to their every beat
Eager to place them all on pedestals
While ignoring those with Beautiful feet!

Yes, the feet of God's chosen prophets
The ones whose mouth contains good news
If only they all were highly regarded
With large crowds packing the pews.

See, they preach the Gospel of Jesus
Living Words to save the soul
They are gifts sent down from Heaven
With glad tidings to make men whole.

Oh, their Feet are Oh So Beautiful
See, they walk by the Saviour's side
When they courageously tell His story
The Master's heart doth beam with pride!

It's a shame their beauty is hidden
And their value so lightly esteemed
For their words have broken men's bondage
And propelled others to achieve their dreams!

Oh, their feet are Oh So Beautiful
Their impact God's saints must tell
Their beautiful words have altered destinies
And snatched many from the gates of Hell!

So when you behold the gospel preacher
May your deeds be kind and sweet
He's a special Gift from Heaven
He's that man with Beautiful Feet!

I'll Use This Day
for Praise

How often do we take for granted that we will see another day? *Because we assume the next day is for certain, we often fail to give proper praise to God for today.* Instead of praising Him, we spend the day complaining about the weather, the work schedule, or the physical discomforts, or we focus on what we don't have. If we can grasp that today is all that we really have, we would recognize it as a gift from God. Therefore, we would be more cognizant to utilize each treasured day as an opportunity to give thanks, to offer praise, and to celebrate the wondrous blessing of life. *This poem offers an encouraging recommendation on how we all should use the blessing of TODAY!*

Psalm 118:24: "This is the DAY which the LORD has made; Let us REJOICE and be GLAD in it."

I'll Use This Day for Praise

Today's a day I've never seen before
One I surely won't see again
So with my mouth I offer up praise
For *ALL* that You have been!

When the dark clouds of life surrounded me
You were my shelter during the storm
With Your wings you graciously covered me
And kept me safe from hurt and harm!

A waymaker and a troubleshooter
You've been those things for me
Your goodness and mercy at my side
As far back as I can see!

Today I'll gladly sing and shout
And Your Greatness I will proclaim
And with this day, I celebrate
The Excellence of Your Name!

Today is all that I have before me
For Yesterday already has passed
Tomorrow is day that I may not see
I will give praise like today is my last!

Can't spend this day complaining
'Cause THIS DAY is my gift from You
I'm going to clap my hands, rejoice, and dance
That's exactly what I'm going do!

Lord, thank you for this Beautiful Day!